DOVER · THRIFT · EDITIONS

Renascence
and
Other Poems

EDNA ST. VINCENT MILLAY

ᴥ

DOVER PUBLICATIONS, INC.
New York

DOVER THRIFT EDITIONS

EDITOR: STANLEY APPELBAUM

This Dover edition, first published in 1991, is an
unabridged republication of the first edition, originally published
by Mitchell Kennerley, New York, in 1917. Added in the Dover edition
are a new Note and alphabetical lists of titles and first lines.

Manufactured in the United States of America
Dover Publications, Inc.
31 East 2nd Street
Mineola, N.Y. 11501

Library of Congress Cataloging-in-Publication Data

Millay, Edna St. Vincent, 1892–1950.
Renascence and other poems / Edna St. Vincent Millay.
p.   cm. — (Dover thrift editions)
Includes indexes.
ISBN 0-486-26873-X (pbk.)
I. Title.   II. Series.
PS3525.I495R4   1991
811'.52—dc20   91-11878
                                                    CIP

Note

Renascence and Other Poems, of 1917, was the first volume of verse published by Edna St. Vincent Millay (1892–1950), American poet, short-story writer, playwright, librettist and actress. The title poem had been printed separately as early as 1912. The sonnet, of which six examples are included here, later became the verse form most closely associated with Millay. She was to win a Pulitzer Prize for poetry in 1923.

Although in the 1920s she was popularly regarded as a cynic, rebel and liberated woman, the simple and direct early works gathered in *Renascence and Other Poems* are more concerned with bereavement and sorrow, alleviated by a love of nature and a continuing search for happiness.

Contents

Renascence
and
Other Poems

Renascence

All I could see from where I stood
Was three long mountains and a wood;
I turned and looked another way,
And saw three islands in a bay.
So with my eyes I traced the line
Of the horizon, thin and fine,
Straight around till I was come
Back to where I'd started from;
And all I saw from where I stood
Was three long mountains and a wood.
Over these things I could not see;
These were the things that bounded me;
And I could touch them with my hand,
Almost, I thought, from where I stand.
And all at once things seemed so small
My breath came short, and scarce at all.
But, sure, the sky is big, I said;
Miles and miles above my head;
So here upon my back I'll lie
And look my fill into the sky.
And so I looked, and, after all,
The sky was not so very tall.
The sky, I said, must somewhere stop,
And—sure enough!—I see the top!

The sky, I thought, is not so grand;
I 'most could touch it with my hand!
And reaching up my hand to try,
I screamed to feel it touch the sky.
I screamed, and—lo!—Infinity
Came down and settled over me;
Forced back my scream into my chest,
Bent back my arm upon my breast,
And, pressing of the Undefined
The definition on my mind,
Held up before my eyes a glass
Through which my shrinking sight did pass
Until it seemed I must behold
Immensity made manifold;
Whispered to me a word whose sound
Deafened the air for worlds around,
And brought unmuffled to my ears
The gossiping of friendly spheres,
The creaking of the tented sky,
The ticking of Eternity.
I saw and heard, and knew at last
The How and Why of all things, past,
And present, and forevermore.
The Universe, cleft to the core,
Lay open to my probing sense
That, sick'ning, I would fain pluck thence
But could not,—nay! But needs must suck
At the great wound, and could not pluck
My lips away till I had drawn

All venom out.—Ah, fearful pawn!
For my omniscience paid I toll
In infinite remorse of soul.
All sin was of my sinning, all
Atoning mine, and mine the gall
Of all regret. Mine was the weight
Of every brooded wrong, the hate
That stood behind each envious thrust,
Mine every greed, mine every lust.
And all the while for every grief,
Each suffering, I craved relief
With individual desire,—
Craved all in vain! And felt fierce fire
About a thousand people crawl;
Perished with each,—then mourned for all!
A man was starving in Capri;
He moved his eyes and looked at me;
I felt his gaze, I heard his moan,
And knew his hunger as my own.
I saw at sea a great fog bank
Between two ships that struck and sank;
A thousand screams the heavens smote;
And every scream tore through my throat.
No hurt I did not feel, no death
That was not mine; mine each last breath
That, crying, met an answering cry
From the compassion that was I.
All suffering mine, and mine its rod;
Mine, pity like the pity of God.

Ah, awful weight! Infinity
Pressed down upon the finite Me!
My anguished spirit, like a bird,
Beating against my lips I heard;
Yet lay the weight so close about
There was no room for it without.
And so beneath the weight lay I
And suffered death, but could not die.

Long had I lain thus, craving death,
When quietly the earth beneath
Gave way, and inch by inch, so great
At last had grown the crushing weight,
Into the earth I sank till I
Full six feet under ground did lie,
And sank no more,—there is no weight
Can follow here, however great.
From off my breast I felt it roll,
And as it went my tortured soul
Burst forth and fled in such a gust
That all about me swirled the dust.

Deep in the earth I rested now;
Cool is its hand upon the brow
And soft its breast beneath the head
Of one who is so gladly dead.
And all at once, and over all
The pitying rain began to fall;
I lay and heard each pattering hoof

Upon my lowly, thatchèd roof,
And seemed to love the sound far more
Than ever I had done before.
For rain it hath a friendly sound
To one who's six feet underground;
And scarce the friendly voice or face:
A grave is such a quiet place.

The rain, I said, is kind to come
And speak to me in my new home.
I would I were alive again
To kiss the fingers of the rain,
To drink into my eyes the shine
Of every slanting silver line,
To catch the freshened, fragrant breeze
From drenched and dripping apple-trees.
For soon the shower will be done,
And then the broad face of the sun
Will laugh above the rain-soaked earth
Until the world with answering mirth
Shakes joyously, and each round drop
Rolls, twinkling, from its grass-blade top.
How can I bear it; buried here,
While overhead the sky grows clear
And blue again after the storm?
O, multi-colored, multiform,
Beloved beauty over me,
That I shall never, never see
Again! Spring-silver, autumn-gold,

That I shall never more behold!
Sleeping your myriad magics through,
Close-sepulchred away from you!
O God, I cried, give me new birth,
And put me back upon the earth!
Upset each cloud's gigantic gourd
And let the heavy rain, down-poured
In one big torrent, set me free,
Washing my grave away from me!

I ceased; and through the breathless hush
That answered me, the far-off rush
Of herald wings came whispering
Like music down the vibrant string
Of my ascending prayer, and—crash!
Before the wild wind's whistling lash
The startled storm-clouds reared on high
And plunged in terror down the sky,
And the big rain in one black wave
Fell from the sky and struck my grave.
I know not how such things can be;
I only know there came to me
A fragrance such as never clings
To aught save happy living things;
A sound as of some joyous elf
Singing sweet songs to please himself,
And, through and over everything,
A sense of glad awakening.
The grass, a-tiptoe at my ear,

Whispering to me I could hear;
I felt the rain's cool finger-tips
Brushed tenderly across my lips,
Laid gently on my sealèd sight,
And all at once the heavy night
Fell from my eyes and I could see,—
A drenched and dripping apple-tree,
A last long line of silver rain,
A sky grown clear and blue again.
And as I looked a quickening gust
Of wind blew up to me and thrust
Into my face a miracle
Of orchard-breath, and with the smell,—
I know not how such things can be!—
I breathed my soul back into me.
Ah! Up then from the ground sprang I
And hailed the earth with such a cry
As is not heard save from a man
Who has been dead, and lives again.
About the trees my arms I wound;
Like one gone mad I hugged the ground;
I raised my quivering arms on high;
I laughed and laughed into the sky,
Till at my throat a strangling sob
Caught fiercely, and a great heart-throb
Sent instant tears into my eyes;
O God, I cried, no dark disguise
Can e'er hereafter hide from me
Thy radiant identity!

Thou canst not move across the grass
But my quick eyes will see Thee pass,
Nor speak, however silently,
But my hushed voice will answer Thee.
I know the path that tells Thy way
Through the cool eve of every day;
God, I can push the grass apart
And lay my finger on Thy heart!

The world stands out on either side
No wider than the heart is wide;
Above the world is stretched the sky,—
No higher than the soul is high.
The heart can push the sea and land
Farther away on either hand;
The soul can split the sky in two,
And let the face of God shine through.
But East and West will pinch the heart
That can not keep them pushed apart;
And he whose soul is flat—the sky
Will cave in on him by and by.

The Suicide

"Curse thee, Life, I will live with thee no more!
Thou hast mocked me, starved me, beat my body sore!
And all for a pledge that was not pledged by me,
I have kissed thy crust and eaten sparingly
That I might eat again, and met thy sneers
With deprecations, and thy blows with tears,—
Aye, from thy glutted lash, glad, crawled away,
As if spent passion were a holiday!
And now I go. Nor threat, nor easy vow
Of tardy kindness can avail thee now
With me, whence fear and faith alike are flown;
Lonely I came, and I depart alone,
And know not where nor unto whom I go;
But that thou canst not follow me I know."

Thus I to Life, and ceased; but through my brain
My thought ran still, until I spake again:

"Ah, but I go not as I came,—no trace
Is mine to bear away of that old grace
I brought! I have been heated in thy fires,
Bent by thy hands, fashioned to thy desires,
Thy mark is on me! I am not the same
Nor ever more shall be, as when I came.

Ashes am I of all that once I seemed.
In me all's sunk that leapt, and all that dreamed
Is wakeful for alarm,—oh, shame to thee,
For the ill change that thou hast wrought in me,
Who laugh no more nor lift my throat to sing!
Ah, Life, I would have been a pleasant thing
To have about the house when I was grown
If thou hadst left my little joys alone!
I asked of thee no favor save this one:
That thou wouldst leave me playing in the sun!
And this thou didst deny, calling my name
Insistently, until I rose and came.
I saw the sun no more.—It were not well
So long on these unpleasant thoughts to dwell,
Need I arise to-morrow and renew
Again my hated tasks, but I am through
With all things save my thoughts and this one night,
So that in truth I seem already quite
Free and remote from thee,—I feel no haste
And no reluctance to depart; I taste
Merely, with thoughtful mien, an unknown draught,
That in a little while I shall have quaffed."

Thus I to Life, and ceased, and slightly smiled,
Looking at nothing; and my thin dreams filed
Before me one by one till once again
I set new words unto an old refrain:

"Treasures thou hast that never have been mine!
Warm lights in many a secret chamber shine

Of thy gaunt house, and gusts of song have blown
Like blossoms out to me that sat alone!
And I have waited well for thee to show
If any share were mine,—and now I go!
Nothing I leave, and if I naught attain
I shall but come into mine own again!"
Thus I to Life, and ceased, and spake no more,
But turning, straightway, sought a certain door
In the rear wall. Heavy it was, and low
And dark,—a way by which none e'er would go
That other exit had, and never knock
Was heard thereat,—bearing a curious lock
Some chance had shown me fashioned faultily,
Whereof Life held content the useless key,
And great coarse hinges, thick and rough with rust,
Whose sudden voice across a silence must,
I knew, be harsh and horrible to hear,—
A strange door, ugly like a dwarf.—So near
I came I felt upon my feet the chill
Of acid wind creeping across the sill.
So stood longtime, till over me at last
Came weariness, and all things other passed
To make it room; the still night drifted deep
Like snow about me, and I longed for sleep.

But, suddenly, marking the morning hour,
Bayed the deep-throated bell within the tower!
Startled, I raised my head,—and with a shout
Laid hold upon the latch,—and was without.

*   *   *   *

Ah, long-forgotten, well-remembered road,
Leading me back unto my old abode,
My father's house! There in the night I came,
And found them feasting, and all things the same
As they had been before. A splendour hung
Upon the walls, and such sweet songs were sung
As, echoing out of very long ago,
Had called me from the house of Life, I know.
So fair their raiment shone I looked in shame
On the unlovely garb in which I came;
Then straightway at my hesitancy mocked:
"It is my father's house!" I said and knocked;
And the door opened. To the shining crowd
Tattered and dark I entered, like a cloud,
Seeing no face but his; to him I crept,
And "Father!" I cried, and clasped his knees, and wept.
Ah, days of joy that followed! All alone
I wandered through the house. My own, my own,
My own to touch, my own to taste and smell,
All I had lacked so long and loved so well!
None shook me out of sleep, nor hushed my song,
Nor called me in from the sunlight all day long.

I know not when the wonder came to me
Of what my father's business might be,
And whither fared and on what errands bent
The tall and gracious messengers he sent.

Yet one day with no song from dawn till night
Wondering, I sat, and watched them out of sight.
And the next day I called; and on the third
Asked them if I might go,—but no one heard.
Then, sick with longing, I arose at last
And went unto my father,—in that vast
Chamber wherein he for so many years
Has sat, surrounded by his charts and spheres.
"Father," I said, "Father, I cannot play
The harp that thou didst give me, and all day
I sit in idleness, while to and fro
About me thy serene, grave servants go;
And I am weary of my lonely ease.
Better a perilous journey overseas
Away from thee, than this, the life I lead,
To sit all day in the sunshine like a weed
That grows to naught,—I love thee more than they
Who serve thee most; yet serve thee in no way.
Father, I beg of thee a little task
To dignify my days,—'tis all I ask
Forever, but forever, this denied,
I perish."

     "Child," my father's voice replied,
"All things thy fancy hath desired of me
Thou hast received. I have prepared for thee
Within my house a spacious chamber, where
Are delicate things to handle and to wear,
And all these things are thine. Dost thou love song?
My minstrels shall attend thee all day long.

Or sigh for flowers? My fairest gardens stand
Open as fields to thee on every hand.
And all thy days this word shall hold the same:
No pleasure shalt thou lack that thou shalt name.
But as for tasks—" he smiled, and shook his head;
"Thou hadst thy task, and laidst it by," he said.

God's World

O world, I cannot hold thee close enough!
   Thy winds, thy wide grey skies!
   Thy mists, that roll and rise!
Thy woods, this autumn day, that ache and sag
And all but cry with colour! That gaunt crag
To crush! To lift the lean of that black bluff!
World, World, I cannot get thee close enough!

Long have I known a glory in it all,
         But never knew I this;
         Here such a passion is
As stretcheth me apart,—Lord, I do fear
Thou'st made the world too beautiful this year;
My soul is all but out of me,—let fall
No burning leaf; prithee, let no bird call.

Afternoon on a Hill

I will be the gladdest thing
   Under the sun!
I will touch a hundred flowers
   And not pick one.

I will look at cliffs and clouds
   With quiet eyes,
Watch the wind bow down the grass,
   And the grass rise.

And when lights begin to show
   Up from the town,
I will mark which must be mine,
   And then start down!

Sorrow

Sorrow like a ceaseless rain
   Beats upon my heart.
People twist and scream in pain,—
Dawn will find them still again;
This has neither wax nor wane,
   Neither stop nor start.

People dress and go to town;
   I sit in my chair.
All my thoughts are slow and brown:
Standing up or sitting down
Little matters, or what gown
   Or what shoes I wear.

Tavern

I'll keep a little tavern
    Below the high hill's crest,
Wherein all grey-eyed people
    May set them down and rest.

There shall be plates a-plenty,
    And mugs to melt the chill
Of all the grey-eyed people
    Who happen up the hill.

There sound will sleep the traveller,
    And dream his journey's end,
But I will rouse at midnight
    The falling fire to tend.

Aye, 'tis a curious fancy—
    But all the good I know
Was taught me out of two grey eyes
    A long time ago.

Ashes of Life

Love has gone and left me and the days are all alike;
  Eat I must, and sleep I will,—and would that night were
    here!
But ah!—to lie awake and hear the slow hours strike!
  Would that it were day again!—with twilight near!

Love has gone and left me and I don't know what to do;
  This or that or what you will is all the same to me;
But all the things that I begin I leave before I'm through,—
  There's little use in anything as far as I can see.

Love has gone and left me,—and the neighbors knock and
    borrow,
  And life goes on forever like the gnawing of a mouse,—
And to-morrow and to-morrow and to-morrow and to-morrow
  There's this little street and this little house.

The Little Ghost

I knew her for a little ghost
   That in my garden walked;
The wall is high—higher than most—
   And the green gate was locked.

And yet I did not think of that
   Till after she was gone—
I knew her by the broad white hat,
   All ruffled, she had on.

By the dear ruffles round her feet,
   By her small hands that hung
In their lace mitts, austere and sweet,
   Her gown's white folds among.

I watched to see if she would stay,
   What she would do—and oh!
She looked as if she liked the way
   I let my garden grow!

She bent above my favourite mint
   With conscious garden grace,
She smiled and smiled—there was no hint
   Of sadness in her face.

She held her gown on either side
  To let her slippers show,
And up the walk she went with pride,
  The way great ladies go.

And where the wall is built in new
  And is of ivy bare
She paused—then opened and passed through
  A gate that once was there.

Kin to Sorrow

Am I kin to Sorrow,
　　That so oft
Falls the knocker of my door—
　　Neither loud nor soft,
But as long accustomed,
　　Under Sorrow's hand?
Marigolds around the step
　　And rosemary stand,
And then comes Sorrow—
　　And what does Sorrow care
For the rosemary
　　Or the marigolds there?
Am I kin to Sorrow?
　　Are we kin?
That so oft upon my door—
　　Oh, come in!

Three Songs of Shattering

I

The first rose on my rose-tree
   Budded, bloomed, and shattered,
During sad days when to me
      Nothing mattered.

Grief of grief has drained me clean;
   Still it seems a pity
No one saw,—it must have been
      Very pretty.

II

Let the little birds sing;
   Let the little lambs play;
Spring is here; and so 'tis spring;—
   But not in the old way!

I recall a place
   Where a plum-tree grew;
There you lifted up your face,
   And blossoms covered you.

If the little birds sing,
   And the little lambs play,

Spring is here; and so 'tis spring—
But not in the old way!

III

All the dog-wood blossoms are underneath the tree!
　　Ere spring was going—ah, spring is gone!
And there comes no summer to the like of you and me,—
　　Blossom time is early, but no fruit sets on.

All the dog-wood blossoms are underneath the tree,
　　Browned at the edges, turned in a day;
And I would with all my heart they trimmed a mound for me,
　　And weeds were tall on all the paths that led that way!

The Shroud

Death, I say, my heart is bowed
   Unto thine,—O mother!
This red gown will make a shroud
   Good as any other!

(I, that would not wait to wear
   My own bridal things,
In a dress dark as my hair
   Made my answerings.

I, to-night, that till he came
   Could not, could not wait,
In a gown as bright as flame
   Held for them the gate.)

Death, I say, my heart is bowed
   Unto thine,—O mother!
This red gown will make a shroud
   Good as any other!

The Dream

Love, if I weep it will not matter,
   And if you laugh I shall not care;
Foolish am I to think about it,
   But it is good to feel you there.

Love, in my sleep I dreamed of waking,—
   White and awful the moonlight reached
Over the floor, and somewhere, somewhere,
   There was a shutter loose,—it screeched!

Swung in the wind,—and no wind blowing!—
   I was afraid, and turned to you,
Put out my hand to you for comfort,—
   And you were gone! Cold, cold as dew,

Under my hand the moonlight lay!
   Love, if you laugh I shall not care,
But if I weep it will not matter,—
   Ah, it is good to feel you there!

Indifference

I said,—for Love was laggard, O, Love was slow to come,—
  "I'll hear his step and know his step when I am warm in
    bed;
But I'll never leave my pillow, though there be some
  As would let him in—and take him in with tears!" I said.
I lay,—for Love was laggard, O, he came not until dawn,—
  I lay and listened for his step and could not get to sleep;
And he found me at my window with my big cloak on,
  All sorry with the tears some folks might weep!

Witch-Wife

She is neither pink nor pale,
  And she never will be all mine;
She learned her hands in a fairy-tale,
  And her mouth on a valentine.

She has more hair than she needs;
  In the sun 'tis a woe to me!
And her voice is a string of colored beads,
  Or steps leading into the sea.

She loves me all that she can,
  And her ways to my ways resign;
But she was not made for any man,
  And she never will be all mine.

Blight

Hard seeds of hate I planted
   That should by now be grown,—
Rough stalks, and from thick stamens
   A poisonous pollen blown,
And odors rank, unbreathable,
   From dark corollas thrown!

At dawn from my damp garden
   I shook the chilly dew;
The thin boughs locked behind me
   That sprang to let me through;
The blossoms slept,—I sought a place
   Where nothing lovely grew.

And there, when day was breaking,
   I knelt and looked around:
The light was near, the silence
   Was palpitant with sound;
I drew my hate from out my breast
   And thrust it in the ground.

Oh, ye so fiercely tended,
   Ye little seeds of hate!
I bent above your growing

Early and noon and late,
Yet are ye drooped and pitiful,—
   I cannot rear ye straight!

The sun seeks out my garden,
   No nook is left in shade,
No mist nor mold nor mildew
   Endures on any blade,
Sweet rain slants under every bough:
   Ye falter, and ye fade.

When the Year Grows Old

I cannot but remember
    When the year grows old—
October—November—
    How she disliked the cold!

She used to watch the swallows
    Go down across the sky,
And turn from the window
    With a little sharp sigh.

And often when the brown leaves
    Were brittle on the ground,
And the wind in the chimney
    Made a melancholy sound,

She had a look about her
    That I wish I could forget—
The look of a scared thing
    Sitting in a net!

Oh, beautiful at nightfall
    The soft spitting snow!
And beautiful the bare boughs
    Rubbing to and fro!

But the roaring of the fire,
    And the warmth of fur,
And the boiling of the kettle
    Were beautiful to her!

I cannot but remember
    When the year grows old—
October—November—
    How she disliked the cold!

Sonnets

I

Thou art not lovelier than lilacs,—no,
  Nor honeysuckle; thou art not more fair
  Than small white single poppies,—I can bear
Thy beauty; though I bend before thee, though
From left to right, not knowing where to go,
  I turn my troubled eyes, nor here nor there
  Find any refuge from thee, yet I swear
So has it been with mist,—with moonlight so.

Like him who day by day unto his draught
  Of delicate poison adds him one drop more
Till he may drink unharmed the death of ten,
Even so, inured to beauty, who have quaffed
  Each hour more deeply than the hour before,
I drink—and live—what has destroyed some men.

II

Time does not bring relief; you all have lied
  Who told me time would ease me of my pain!
  I miss him in the weeping of the rain;
I want him at the shrinking of the tide;
The old snows melt from every mountain-side,
  And last year's leaves are smoke in every lane;

But last year's bitter loving must remain
Heaped on my heart, and my old thoughts abide!

There are a hundred places where I fear
    To go,—so with his memory they brim!
And entering with relief some quiet place
Where never fell his foot or shone his face
I say, "There is no memory of him here!"
    And so stand stricken, so remembering him!

III

Mindful of you the sodden earth in spring,
    And all the flowers that in the springtime grow,
    And dusty roads, and thistles, and the slow
Rising of the round moon, all throats that sing
The summer through, and each departing wing,
    And all the nests that the bared branches show,
    And all winds that in any weather blow,
And all the storms that the four seasons bring.

You go no more on your exultant feet
    Up paths that only mist and morning knew,
Or watch the wind, or listen to the beat
    Of a bird's wings too high in air to view,—
But you were something more than young and sweet
    And fair,—and the long year remembers you.

IV

Not in this chamber only at my birth—
    When the long hours of that mysterious night

Were over, and the morning was in sight—
I cried, but in strange places, steppe and firth
I have not seen, through alien grief and mirth;
   And never shall one room contain me quite
   Who in so many rooms first saw the light,
Child of all mothers, native of the earth.

So is no warmth for me at any fire
   To-day, when the world's fire has burned so low;
I kneel, spending my breath in vain desire,
At that cold hearth which one time roared so strong,
And straighten back in weariness, and long
   To gather up my little gods and go.

V

If I should learn, in some quite casual way,
   That you were gone, not to return again—
Read from the back-page of a paper, say,
   Held by a neighbor in a subway train,
How at the corner of this avenue
   And such a street (so are the papers filled)
A hurrying man—who happened to be you—
   At noon to-day had happened to be killed,
I should not cry aloud—I could not cry
   Aloud, or wring my hands in such a place—
I should but watch the station lights rush by
   With a more careful interest on my face,
Or raise my eyes and read with greater care
Where to store furs and how to treat the hair.

VI

Bluebeard

This door you might not open, and you did;
   So enter now, and see for what slight thing
You are betrayed. . . . Here is no treasure hid,
   No cauldron, no clear crystal mirroring
The sought-for truth, no heads of women slain
   For greed like yours, no writhings of distress,
But only what you see. . . . Look yet again—
   An empty room, cobwebbed and comfortless.
Yet this alone out of my life I kept
   Unto myself, lest any know me quite;
And you did so profane me when you crept
   Unto the threshold of this room to-night
That I must never more behold your face.
   This now is yours. I seek another place.

Alphabetical Lists of
Titles and First Lines

Alphabetical List of Titles

Alphabetical List of First Lines

DOVER·THRIFT·EDITIONS

All books complete and unabridged. All 5³⁄₁₆″ × 8¹⁄₄″, paperbound.
Just $1.00–$2.00 in U.S.A.

POETRY

DOVER BEACH AND OTHER POEMS, Matthew Arnold. 112pp. 28037-3 $1.00

BHAGAVADGITA, Bhagavadgita. 112pp. 27782-8 $1.00

SONGS OF INNOCENCE AND SONGS OF EXPERIENCE, William Blake. 64pp. 27051-3 $1.00

SONNETS FROM THE PORTUGUESE AND OTHER POEMS, Elizabeth Barrett Browning. 64pp. 27052-1 $1.00

MY LAST DUCHESS AND OTHER POEMS, Robert Browning. 128pp. 27783-6 $1.00

POEMS AND SONGS, Robert Burns. 96pp. 26863-2 $1.00

SELECTED POEMS, George Gordon, Lord Byron. 112pp. 27784-4 $1.00

THE RIME OF THE ANCIENT MARINER AND OTHER POEMS, Samuel Taylor Coleridge. 80pp. 27266-4 $1.00

SELECTED POEMS, Emily Dickinson. 64pp. 26466-1 $1.00

SELECTED POEMS, John Donne. 96pp. 27788-7 $1.00

THE RUBÁIYÁT OF OMAR KHAYYÁM: FIRST AND FIFTH EDITIONS, Edward FitzGerald. 64pp. 26467-X $1.00

A BOY'S WILL AND NORTH OF BOSTON, Robert Frost. 112pp. (Available in U.S. only.) 26866-7 $1.00

THE ROAD NOT TAKEN AND OTHER POEMS, Robert Frost. 64pp. (Available in U.S. only) 27550-7 $1.00

A SHROPSHIRE LAD, A. E. Housman. 64pp. 26468-8 $1.00

LYRIC POEMS, John Keats. 80pp. 26871-3 $1.00

THE BOOK OF PSALMS, King James Bible. 128pp. 27541-8 $1.00

GUNGA DIN AND OTHER FAVORITE POEMS, Rudyard Kipling. 80pp. 26471-8 $1.00

THE CONGO AND OTHER POEMS, Vachel Lindsay. 96pp. 27272-9 $1.00

FAVORITE POEMS, Henry Wadsworth Longfellow. 96pp. 27273-7 $1.00

SPOON RIVER ANTHOLOGY, Edgar Lee Masters. 144pp. 27275-3 $1.00

RENASCENCE AND OTHER POEMS, Edna St. Vincent Millay. 64pp. (Available in U.S. only.) 26873-X $1.00

SELECTED POEMS, John Milton. 128pp. 27554-X $1.00

GREAT SONNETS, Paul Negri (ed.). 96pp. 28052-7 $1.00

THE RAVEN AND OTHER FAVORITE POEMS, Edgar Allan Poe. 64pp. 26685-0 $1.00

ESSAY ON MAN AND OTHER POEMS, Alexander Pope. 128pp. 28053-5 $1.00

GOBLIN MARKET AND OTHER POEMS, Christina Rossetti. 64pp. 28055-1 $1.00

CHICAGO POEMS, Carl Sandburg. 80pp. 28057-8 $1.00

THE SHOOTING OF DAN MCGREW AND OTHER POEMS, Robert Service. 96pp. 27556-6 $1.00

COMPLETE SONGS FROM THE PLAYS, William Shakespeare. 80pp. 27801-8 $1.00

COMPLETE SONNETS, William Shakespeare. 80pp. 26686-9 $1.00

SELECTED POEMS, Percy Bysshe Shelley. 128pp. 27558-2 $1.00

SELECTED POEMS, Alfred Lord Tennyson. 112pp. 27282-6 $1.00

CHRISTMAS CAROLS: COMPLETE VERSES, Shane Weller (ed.). 64pp. 27397-0 $1.00

DOVER · THRIFT · EDITIONS

All books complete and unabridged. All 5³⁄₁₆″ × 8¼″, paperbound.
Just $1.00–$2.00 in U.S.A.

FICTION

THE MAN WHO WOULD BE KING AND OTHER STORIES, Rudyard Kipling. 128pp. 28051-9 $1.00

SELECTED SHORT STORIES, D. H. Lawrence. 128pp. 27794-1 $1.00

GREEN TEA AND OTHER GHOST STORIES, J. Sheridan LeFanu. 96pp. 27795-X $1.00

THE CALL OF THE WILD, Jack London. 64pp. 26472-6 $1.00

FIVE GREAT SHORT STORIES, Jack London. 96pp. 27063-7 $1.00

WHITE FANG, Jack London. 160pp. 26968-X $1.00

THE NECKLACE AND OTHER SHORT STORIES, Guy de Maupassant. 128pp. 27064-5 $1.00

BARTLEBY AND BENITO CERENO, Herman Melville. 112pp. 26473-4 $1.00

THE GOLD-BUG AND OTHER TALES, Edgar Allan Poe. 128pp. 26875-6 $1.00

THE QUEEN OF SPADES AND OTHER STORIES, Alexander Pushkin. 128pp. 28054-3 $1.00

THREE LIVES, Gertrude Stein. 176pp. 28059-4 $2.00

THE STRANGE CASE OF DR. JEKYLL AND MR. HYDE, Robert Louis Stevenson. 64pp. 26688-5 $1.00

TREASURE ISLAND, Robert Louis Stevenson. 160pp. 27559-0 $1.00

THE KREUTZER SONATA AND OTHER SHORT STORIES, Leo Tolstoy. 144pp. 27805-0 $1.00

ADVENTURES OF HUCKLEBERRY FINN, Mark Twain. 224pp. 28061-6 $2.00

THE MYSTERIOUS STRANGER AND OTHER STORIES, Mark Twain. 128pp. 27069-6 $1.00

CANDIDE, Voltaire (François-Marie Arouet). 112pp. 26689-3 $1.00

THE INVISIBLE MAN, H. G. Wells. 112pp. (Available in U.S. only.) 27071-8 $1.00

ETHAN FROME, Edith Wharton. 96pp. 26690-7 $1.00

THE PICTURE OF DORIAN GRAY, Oscar Wilde. 192pp. 27807-7 $1.00

NONFICTION

THE DEVIL'S DICTIONARY, Ambrose Bierce. 144pp. 27542-6 $1.00

THE SOULS OF BLACK FOLK, W. E. B. Du Bois. 176pp. 28041-1 $2.00

SELF-RELIANCE AND OTHER ESSAYS, Ralph Waldo Emerson. 128pp. 27790-9 $1.00

GREAT SPEECHES, Abraham Lincoln. 112pp. 26872-1 $1.00

THE PRINCE, Niccolò Machiavelli. 80pp. 27274-5 $1.00

SYMPOSIUM AND PHAEDRUS, Plato. 96pp. 27798-4 $1.00

THE TRIAL AND DEATH OF SOCRATES: FOUR DIALOGUES, Plato. 128pp. 27066-1 $1.00

CIVIL DISOBEDIENCE AND OTHER ESSAYS, Henry David Thoreau. 96pp. 27563-9 $1.00

THE THEORY OF THE LEISURE CLASS, Thorstein Veblen. 256pp. 28062-4 $2.00

PLAYS

THE CHERRY ORCHARD, Anton Chekhov. 64pp. 26682-6 $1.00

THE THREE SISTERS, Anton Chekhov. 64pp. 27544-2 $1.00

THE WAY OF THE WORLD, William Congreve. 80pp. 27787-9 $1.00

MEDEA, Euripides. 64pp. 27548-5 $1.00

THE MIKADO, William Schwenck Gilbert. 64pp. 27268-0 $1.00